DISCARDED

Mail Carriers/Carteros

By JoAnn Early Macken

Reading consultant: Susan Nations, M.Ed., author/literacy coach/consultant

Gareth Stevens
Publishing

Please visit our Web site www.garethstevens.com. For a free color catalog of all our high-quality books, call toll free 1-800-542-2595 or fax 1-877-542-2596.

Cataloging Data

Macken, JoAnn Early, 1953-
    Mail carriers / Carteros by JoAnn Early Macken.
      p. cm. — (People in my community)
    Summary: Photographs and simple text describe the work done by mail carriers. Bilingual Edition.
    Includes bibliographical references and index.
    ISBN: 978-1-4339-3763-7 (pbk.)
    ISBN: 978-1-4339-3764-4 (6-pack)
    ISBN: 978-1-4339-3762-0 (library binding)
    1. Letter carriers—United States—Juvenile literature. [1. Letter carriers.   2. Occupations.   3. Spanish-language materials]
  I. Title.   II. Series.

New edition published 2010 by
Gareth Stevens Publishing
111 East 14th Street, Suite 349
New York, NY 10003

New text and images this edition copyright © 2010 Gareth Stevens Publishing

Original edition published 2003 by Weekly Reader® Books
An imprint of Gareth Stevens Publishing
Original edition text and images copyright © 2003 Gareth Stevens Publishing

Art direction: Haley Harasymiw, Tammy Gruenewald
Page layout: Michael Flynn, Katherine A. Goedheer
Editorial direction: Kerri O'Donnell, Diane Laska Swanke
Spanish translation: Eduardo Alamán

Cover, back cover, p. 1 © Jeff Dunn/Photolibrary/Getty Images; p. 5 © Kim Steele/Photodisc/ Getty Images; pp. 7, 9, 11, 13, 15, 17, 21 by Gregg Andersen; p. 19 © Tim Boyle/Getty Images.

Printed in the United States of America

CPSIA compliance information: Batch #WW10GS: For further information contact Gareth Stevens, New York, New York at 1-800-542-2595.

Table of Contents

Contenido

Boldface words appear in the glossary/
Las palabras en **negrita** aparecen en el glosario

Here Comes the Mail!

A mail carrier delivers
the mail.

¡Ya llegó el correo!

Los carteros entregan el correo.

First, mail carriers **sort** the mail at the post office.

Primero, los carteros **separan** el correo en la oficina postal.

Each letter and **package** must go to the right **address**. Mail can be delivered only if it has a **stamp**.

Las cartas y los **paquetes** deben ir a la **dirección** correcta. El correo debe tener una **estampilla**.

address/dirección

Some mail carriers walk to deliver the mail. They might carry the mail in a pouch.

Algunos carteros entregan el correo a pie. Estos carteros usan una bolsa.

pouch/bolsa

Some mail carriers drive cars or trucks to deliver the mail. They drive from house to house.

Otros carteros usan un camión para entregar el correo. Estos manejan de casa en casa.

truck/camión

2208844

Some mail carriers have the same **route** each day. They deliver mail to homes, businesses, and schools.

Algunos carteros tienen la misma **ruta** todos los días. Estos carteros llevan el correo a casas, oficinas y escuelas.

Special Clothes

Mail carriers wear special **uniforms**. In the summer, they may wear shorts.

Ropa especial

Los carteros usan un **uniforme** especial. En el verano, algunos usan pantalones cortos.

uniform/uniforme

UNITED STATES
POSTAL SERVICE

17

In the winter, they wear warmer clothes. Mail carriers work in all kinds of weather.

- - - - - - - - - - - - - - - - - - - -

En el invierno usan ropa abrigadora. Los carteros trabajan en todos los climas.

Mail for Me!

It's fun to get something in the mail!

- -

¡Una carta para mí!

¡Es muy divertido recibir cartas por correo!

Glossary/Glosario

address: the place where mail gets delivered

package: a box or carton with things packed in it

route: a path taken from place to place

sort: to put in order

stamp: something put on mail to show that you paid to send it

uniform: clothing worn by members of a group such as police officers, firefighters, or mail carriers

----

dirección (la) el lugar al que se envía el correo

estampilla (la) Una estampa que se pone en el correo para probar que se ha pagado

paquete (el) una caja de cartón con cosas dentro

ruta (la) el camino que se toma para ir de un lugar a otro

separar poner en orden

uniforme (el) ropa especial que usan los policías, carteros o bomberos